101 TRIVIA QUESTIONS ABOUT CRISTIANO RONALDO

A BIOGRAPHY OF ESSENTIAL FACTS AND STORIES YOU NEED TO KNOW!

FAME FOCUS

CONTENTS

INTRODUCTION

Welcome to *101 Trivia Questions About Cristiano Ronaldo!* This book is a treasure trove of fascinating insights, stories, and trivia about one of the most iconic figures in the world of soccer, Cristiano Ronaldo. As a player who has mesmerized fans with his skills, determination, and remarkable achievements on the soccer pitch, Ronaldo's journey from the humble streets of Madeira to global stardom is nothing short of inspirational.

Embark on a journey through the life of a soccer legend, exploring his early days, illustrious career, personal life, and the impact he has made both on and off the field. Each trivia question in this book is carefully crafted to test your knowledge and deepen your understanding of this extraordinary athlete.

Ronaldo, a living legend in the world of soccer, is still actively writing his extraordinary story. This book was finished in October 2023. He continues to captivate audiences and set new standards in the sport. It's important to note that the facts and statistics within this book are accurate as of this date. With his career ongoing, Ronaldo's journey is an evolving saga, promising the possibility of more records to be shattered and more exhilarating chapters yet to unfold.

Get ready to dive into the world of Cristiano Ronaldo, a journey through the life of a man who has become more than just a soccer player, but a symbol of dedication, excellence, and unparalleled success.

1

INSIDE THE WORLD OF SOCCER

Before we dive into Cristiano Ronaldo's remarkable journey in soccer, it's important to first understand the wider soccer world that has been a stage for his impressive career. In this section, we'll look at the key parts of soccer that have been a backdrop to his story. We'll explore the importance of the Ballon d'Or, the excitement of La Liga, the prestige of the UEFA

European Championship, the passion of El Clásico, the global appeal of the FIFA World Cup, the energy of the Premier League, and the two big championships of Spain: Copa del Rey and Supercopa de España. Grasping the significance of these competitions and awards is essential to fully appreciating Ronaldo's journey and successes. They are more than just tournaments or prizes; they represent the highest levels of a sport loved by millions around the world. As we talk about Ronaldo in the following pages, understanding this background will help us see the full scope of his influence on soccer and its celebrated history.

Ballon d'Or

The Ballon d'Or is one of the most prestigious individual awards in the world of soccer. It's an annual accolade presented by France Football magazine to the best male soccerer in the world, as voted on by a panel of international journalists, national team coaches, national team captains, and managers.

The award has a long history, dating back to 1956 when it was first introduced. Originally, it was limited to European players playing for European clubs, but the eligibility criteria were expanded to include players from all around the world, regardless of where they play, in 1995.

The Ballon d'Or recognizes outstanding individual performances in a calendar year, taking into account a player's contributions to their club and national team. The criteria for selecting the winner include skill, consistency, leadership, and impact on the game. The award is a symbol of excellence in soccer and is highly coveted by players, as it represents recognition of their talent and achievements on the field.

El Clásico

"El Clásico" is more than just a soccer match; it's a legendary rivalry between FC Barcelona and Real Madrid, representing a historic and intense contest that has captivated fans since the early 20th century. This rivalry, known for being one of the most anticipated in world soccer, involves much more than the sport itself. Matches between Barcelona and Real Madrid are global events, marked by high stakes, intense emotions, and unparalleled competition. These games are cultural phenomena that often divide families, cities, and even nations along soccering lines.

The global appeal of "El Clásico" is immense, drawing attention from fans around the world. It's not only a display of extraordinary player talent but also a showcase of the unique soccering philosophies and traditions of the two clubs. The rivalry has been graced by soccer legends like Lionel Messi, Alfredo Di Stéfano, and Johan Cruyff, each adding to the match's prestige with memorable performances.

Beyond the pitch, "El Clásico" holds significant cultural importance in Spain, embodying the nation's diverse identities. Barcelona and Real Madrid represent more than just soccer clubs; they symbolize regional pride and political nuances, with Barcelona often associated with Catalonia and Real Madrid with the Spanish capital.

The matches are events where passion, skill, and drama converge, captivating both soccer enthusiasts and casual viewers. Whether played at Barcelona's Camp Nou or Madrid's Santiago Bernabéu, these stadiums transform into stages where some of soccer's greatest stories unfold, making "El Clásico" a true spectacle in the world of sports.

Premier League

The Premier League, established in 1992, is England's elite professional soccer league and one of the world's most historic and widely followed soccer competitions. It has become a hallmark of English  soccer, known for its global appeal and competitive nature.

Featuring 20 clubs, the Premier League's season runs from August to May, with each club playing 38 matches against all others, both home and away. Celebrated for its diversity and unpredictability, the league sees a blend of varying styles and philosophies, leading to a dynamic and thrilling brand of soccer. Known for its fast-paced, end-to-end play, the Premier League is especially noted for its focus on attacking soccer.

The league has cultivated an enormous international following, attracting fans globally with its high production values, extensive broadcasting, and world-class talent, making it one of the most-watched sports leagues worldwide. Iconic clubs like Manchester United, Liverpool, Chelsea, Arsenal, and Manchester City, each with fervent fan bases, add to the league's allure. Historic rivalries, such as the "North West Derby" between Liverpool and Manchester United, inject additional drama and history into the league.

Premier League clubs have consistently shown excellence in European competitions, often featuring prominently in the UEFA Champions League and UEFA Europa League. Beyond the field, the Premier League is deeply embedded in English culture and society, resonating with millions of fans. Soccer forms an integral part of the nation's heritage, with Premier League matches being of great significance to local communities.

La Liga

La Liga, or the Spanish Football League, has a storied history that spans nearly a century, tracing its roots back to its establishment in 1929. It stands as one of Europe's oldest soccer leagues, steeped in tradition and significance within the Spanish soccer landscape.

La Liga consists of 20 teams that undergo a rigorous season from August to May, each team playing 38 matches - one at home and one away against every other team. Scoring in this league is based on wins (three points), draws (one point), and losses (zero points), all contributing to the race for the championship. Known for its captivating and technical style of play, La Liga is home to famous clubs like FC Barcelona and Real Madrid, whose intense rivalry in "El Clásico" attracts global attention. The league's appeal extends far beyond Spain, captivating fans worldwide with its top-tier talent and high-quality soccer. On the European stage, La Liga clubs, including Barcelona, Real Madrid, and Atletico Madrid, have consistently excelled, cementing their status as European soccer powerhouses in tournaments like the UEFA Champions League and UEFA Europa League. Within Spain, La Liga holds a significant cultural place, with soccer being a deeply rooted passion. League matches are a key part of the country's sports and social calendar, underlining soccer's profound influence on Spanish society. Furthermore, La Liga has been instrumental in expanding soccer's popularity globally, propelling Spanish soccer to a prominent position and spreading the love for the game to various corners of the world.

UEFA European Championship

Since its first edition in 1960, the UEFA European Championship, commonly known as the Euro, has been a pivotal event in the world of soccer, captivating fans with its rich history and showcasing Europe's finest national teams. As one of the most esteemed international soccer competitions, it has evolved significantly over the years. The competition format of the modern Euro includes 24 top national teams from UEFA member countries, divided into groups and then proceeding to knockout stages, culminating in the crowning of the European champion. The Euro is celebrated for its intense matches, tactical prowess, and the emergence of new soccer heroes, offering a stage where national pride and passion reach their zenith, creating unforgettable moments.

While the Euro is a European event, its appeal extends globally, attracting soccer enthusiasts worldwide. Its high-level play and world-class talent make it a highlight of the international soccer calendar. Over the years, the championship has witnessed a variety of winners, from soccer giants to unexpected underdogs, each contributing to the diverse tapestry of European soccer. More than just a sporting competition, the Euro holds a special place in European culture, symbolizing a celebration that unites nations and communities, fostering unity and pride. On the international soccer stage, the Euro's impact is profound. It offers teams a chance to compete against the best, with success in the tournament becoming a source of national pride and glory, thus playing a significant role in shaping the international soccer landscape.

FIFA World Cup

The FIFA World Cup represents the zenith of international soccer, having established itself as a historic and beloved event since its inception in 1930. Renowned as the most prestigious and widely  viewed sporting event globally, the World Cup showcases top national teams from every continent.

More than just a soccer tournament, the World Cup is a worldwide celebration of the sport. Held quadrennially, it unites nations, cultures, and people from diverse backgrounds in their shared passion for soccer. This period is marked by a global pause, as soccer fever sweeps through countries, captivating the attention of people worldwide.

The competition within the World Cup is intense. Teams engage in a month-long contest that is a testament to national pride, with players showcasing their talent on the world's biggest stage. The format of the tournament encompasses group stages, knockout rounds, and culminates in the final, with each match carrying the potential to make history.

The World Cup has been the arena for the emergence of legendary players who have significantly influenced the sport. Icons such as Pelé, and Diego Maradona have graced this tournament, demonstrating extraordinary soccering prowess.

Beyond the realm of sports, the World Cup has a profound cultural impact. It fosters unity and camaraderie, often bringing together rival nations in a shared celebration. The event also allows host countries the opportunity to display their culture, traditions, and hospitality to a global audience.

The World Cup transcends being merely a sporting event; it is a global phenomenon. Attracting billions of viewers, sparking passionate discussions, and creating indelible memories, the tournament holds the unique power to inspire and unite people like no other event in the world.

Copa del Rey

The Copa del Rey, translated as the "King's Cup" in Spanish, is a knockout football competition held in Spain and organized by the Royal Spanish Football Federation. Inaugurated in

1903, it stands as one of the oldest football tournaments globally, attracting teams from diverse levels of the Spanish football league system and showcasing a rich array of talent and competition.

The tournament format of the Copa del Rey involves a series of knockout rounds. It traditionally kicks off with single-leg matches in the early stages, transitions to two-legged ties in the later rounds, and culminates in an intense single-match final. This structure adds an element of excitement and unpredictability, often resulting in unexpected outcomes and thrilling moments in Spanish football.

Initially dominated by top-tier teams, the Copa del Rey has expanded its reach to include participation from lower divisions, providing smaller clubs with the opportunity to face off against the powerhouses of Spanish football. This inclusivity adds a special allure to the competition, fostering classic "David vs. Goliath" matchups.

The winner of the Copa del Rey not only claims a prestigious trophy but also typically earns a coveted spot in the UEFA Europa League for the subsequent season, unless they have already secured a place in the UEFA Champions League through their league performance. This dual incentive serves as an extra impetus for clubs to strive for success in the tournament.

Supercopa de España

The Spanish Super Cup, known as the Supercopa de España, has been a prominent fixture in Spanish football since its inception in 1982. Traditionally, the competition brings together the champions of La Liga, the premier football division in Spain, and the winners of the Copa del Rey, the esteemed national cup competition. This tournament, held at the commencement of the football season, serves as a captivating prelude, allowing top teams in Spain to set the tone for the upcoming year.

Initially, the Supercopa de España featured a two-legged format, with each participating team hosting a match at their home ground. However, a significant change occurred in 2019 when the competition expanded to include four teams - the winners and runners-up of both La Liga and the Copa del Rey. The matches are now decided through a single-round knockout format held at a neutral venue, introducing an element of thrill and unpredictability to the proceedings.

The Supercopa de España offers football enthusiasts an early-season spectacle, showcasing intense matchups between football powerhouses like Real Madrid and Barcelona. These games not only display high-quality football but also embody the fierce rivalries and rich history that characterize Spanish football.

Securing victory in the Supercopa de España is highly coveted, representing success against some of the strongest teams in Spanish football. The title is esteemed as a prestigious accolade, serving as an early gauge of a team's form and potential for success in the upcoming season.

2

RONALDO'S LIFE

Family Roots

On the picturesque island of Madeira, Portugal, a story began that would captivate the world of soccer. Cristiano Ronaldo dos Santos Aveiro, a name now synonymous with excellence in the sport, was born on February 5, 1985. His early life, set against the backdrop of the serene Madeiran landscape, was marked by humble beginnings and a tightly-knit family unit.

The youngest of four children, Ronaldo was cradled in the nurturing hands of Maria Dolores dos Santos Aveiro and José Dinis Aveiro. Dolores, a hardworking cook, was the pillar of strength and encouragement, fostering young Ronaldo's burgeoning talents. She was the force behind his relentless pursuit of excellence, often accompanying him to training sessions and matches, ensuring that his talents didn't go unnoticed.

José Dinis Aveiro, Ronaldo's father, juggled roles as a municipal gardener and a part-time kit man for Andorinha, the local soccer club that would be the first to witness Ronaldo's talents. Though his struggles with alcoholism cast a shadow, his influence on Ronaldo's early soccering life was undeniable. Tragically, his battle with alcoholism led to liver failure, resulting in his untimely death in 2005, leaving a void in the young athlete's life.

In the Aveiro household, where the seeds of Ronaldo's future were sown, his older brother Hugo emerged not just as a sibling but as an integral part of the CR7 brand's journey. Hugo's involvement in projects related to Ronaldo's CR7 brand and museum reflects the family's collective pride and contribution to Ronaldo's legacy.

In the Aveiro family, Cristiano wasn't the only one with a flair for the spotlight. His sisters, Elma and Liliana Cátia, carved their own paths. Elma delved into the business world, playing a pivotal role in managing Ronaldo's CR7 fashion brand. Liliana Cátia, also known as Katia Aveiro, channeled her energy into music, becoming a recognized singer in Portugal and releasing several albums. Their diverse talents reflected a family of varied gifts and passions, united in their support for each other.

 The name Cristiano Ronaldo, now echoing in stadiums worldwide, has an interesting origin. Named after Ronald Reagan, his father's favorite actor, the choice reflected a fondness for the actor's strength and charisma, qualities that Cristiano would embody in his own life and career.

As a youngster, Ronaldo was affectionately nicknamed 'Cry Baby' and 'Little Bee.' 'Cry Baby' was a nod to his emotional reaction when his passes on the pitch didn't translate into goals, showing his early passion for success and teamwork. 'Little Bee,' on the other hand, was a testament to his remarkable speed, a characteristic that would become a hallmark of his playing style.

Early Beginnings

Ronaldo's journey in soccer began at the tender age of eight with the amateur team Andorinha in Madeira. His talent was evident even at this young age, setting the stage for a future that would exceed the wildest dreams of the small island club.

Embarking on a transformative journey, Cristiano Ronaldo faced a pivotal moment at the age of 14. The expulsion from school, a consequence of throwing a chair at a teacher in response to perceived disrespect, proved to be a challenging yet defining episode. It marked a turning point in Ronaldo's life, catalyzed by the encouragement of his mother. In the face of adversity, Ronaldo made a decisive choice, redirecting his full attention to soccer. Little did he know that this decision would reshape his destiny, propelling him toward the dazzling heights of global soccer stardom.

Just a year later, at the age of 15, Ronaldo encountered a critical health challenge—Tachycardia, a condition causing a rapid heartbeat. The potential threat to his career was significant, but Ronaldo faced it head-on. Undergoing a swift and successful heart surgery, employing an advanced laser technique, he emerged from the hospital on the same day with undiminished resolve and physical prowess. This unexpected obstacle, instead of hindering his path, became a crucial stepping stone in Ronaldo's remarkable journey.

At the age of 17, Ronaldo's professional soccer career took its initial strides as he made his debut for Sporting CP in Portugal. This marked the culmination of a journey that began as a young boy in Madeira and progressed to him emerging as a rising star in Lisbon's Sporting CP. Throughout this trajectory, Ronaldo's character was defined by resilience, passion, and an unwavering determination to excel on the soccer field.

Rising at Manchester United

In 2003, a new chapter began for Cristiano Ronaldo as his extraordinary talent captured the attention of Manchester United. The English giants secured his signature for a record-breaking £12.24 million ($23.52 million), the highest ever for a teenager at the time, catapulting him into the elite realm of the English Premier League. This monumental move began a transformative era for Ronaldo and the club.

At Manchester United, Ronaldo swiftly became known for his dazzling 'Ronaldo Chop,' a deft step-over move that bewildered defenders and became a signature element of his play. His flair and skill were not just for show; they contributed significantly to the team's success. Ronaldo was instrumental in Manchester United's dominance in the English Premier League, contributing to three consecutive titles in the 2006-07, 2007-08, and 2008-09 seasons. The 2007-08 season was particularly remarkable. Ronaldo's prowess on the field was pivotal in Manchester United clinching the prestigious UEFA Champions League title.

2008 emerged as a defining year in Ronaldo's career. He achieved personal glory by winning his first Ballon d'Or, an accolade affirming his status as the world's best player. That same year, Ronaldo tasted global victory with Manchester United, securing the FIFA Club World Cup.

Real Madrid Era

The year 2009 marked another significant milestone in Ronaldo's career as he made a historic transfer to Real Madrid for a then-world record fee of £80 million. This move shattered transfer records and opened a new chapter of extraordinary achievements in Spain. His nine seasons at Real Madrid were marked by phenomenal success, as he became the club's all-time leading scorer.

Ronaldo's tenure at Real Madrid was laden with silverware, including four impressive Champions League titles. His influence on the pitch was acknowledged globally, earning him the rank of third in the 'World Player of the Decade 2000s,' an accolade placing him among the likes of Lionel Messi and Ronaldinho.

The 2010-11 season saw Ronaldo clinch his first trophy with Real Madrid, winning the Copa del Rey. This victory was not just a triumph for the club but a personal milestone for Ronaldo. In a thrilling final against arch-rivals Barcelona, Ronaldo's spectacular header sealed the win, ending Real Madrid's 18-year drought in the competition and setting a precedent for his future successes with the club.

Continuing his remarkable journey with Real Madrid, Cristiano Ronaldo ushered in the 2011-12 season by clinching his first La Liga title with the club. This achievement was a testament to his relentless pursuit of success and his critical role in driving the team to the pinnacle of Spanish soccer.

Ronaldo's winning streak continued in the 2012-13 season as he helped Real Madrid secure the Supercopa de España. His relentless drive and exceptional skill on the field were pivotal in conquering this Spanish soccer championship.

Ronaldo's brilliance was again recognized globally in the 2013-14 season when he was awarded his second Ballon d'Or, symbolizing his stature as one of the best players in the world. That season further cemented his legacy as he led Real Madrid to another Copa del Rey victory and clinched his second Champions League title. Ronaldo set a staggering record in the Champions League, scoring 17 goals in the tournament, a feat unmatched by any player.

In 2014, Ronaldo's trophy cabinet expanded with the addition of his third Ballon d'Or and his second FIFA Club World Cup, both significant acknowledgments of his prowess and contribution to the sport.

2016 marked yet another milestone in Ronaldo's illustrious career. He won his third Champions League with Real Madrid, playing a decisive role in the final against Atlético Madrid by scoring the winning penalty, further elevating his status as a clutch player in high-stakes matches.

The following season was one of unprecedented success for Ronaldo. He won his fourth Ballon d'Or and, after a five-year wait, added another La Liga title to his accolades. He continued his dominance in European soccer by securing another Champions League trophy and achieved his second Club World Cup, showcasing his extraordinary ability to perform consistently at the highest level.

In the 2017-18 season, his last with Real Madrid, Ronaldo reached new heights by winning his fifth Ballon d'Or in 2017 and clinching his fifth Champions League title. His remarkable performance in the final against Juventus, where he scored twice, was a fitting climax to his time at Real Madrid. Ronaldo set a record as the first player to win the UEFA Champions League five times, a testament to his enduring excellence in European soccer.

Ronaldo's departure from Real Madrid in July 2018 to join Juventus was a significant moment in soccer history. He left as Real Madrid's all-time top goal scorer and the only player in La Liga history to score 30 or more goals in six consecutive seasons, a record that speaks volumes of his relentless goal-scoring ability.

From Juventus Back to Manchester United Again

In the summer of 2018, Cristiano Ronaldo made a groundbreaking move to Juventus, with the transfer amounting to a staggering initial £88 million ($100 million). This marked a historic moment, not only as the most expensive transfer for an Italian club but also as the priciest deal involving a player over 30 years old. Ronaldo's arrival at Juventus sparked a period of unparalleled success, contributing significantly to the club's triumphs, including clinching two Serie A titles, securing two Supercoppa Italiana trophies, and lifting the Coppa Italia.

During his tenure with Juventus, Ronaldo left an indelible mark on the Italian soccer landscape. His exceptional performances were duly recognized when he was bestowed with the inaugural Serie A Most Valuable Player award. Furthermore, Ronaldo etched his name in the annals of soccer history by becoming the first player ever to secure the top scorer position in the English Premier League, La Liga, and Serie A—underscoring his unparalleled prowess across multiple top-tier leagues.

In a surprising twist, Ronaldo made a highly anticipated return to Manchester United in 2021. In his only full season back at the club, he showcased his enduring goal-scoring prowess by finishing as the top scorer. However, in a turn of events, his contract with Manchester United was terminated in 2022, closing a chapter that had brought moments of triumph and a rekindling of the iconic connection between Ronaldo and the Red Devils.

Debut with Al Nassr

In December 2022, Cristiano signed a two-and-a-half-year contract, estimated by the media to be worth more than 200 million euros ($220.16 million), with the Saudi club Al Nassr. He made his debut there in January 2023, marking a new chapter in his career and demonstrating his continued demand in the soccer world.

Performance Alongside Portugal

Parallel to his club career, Ronaldo's international journey with Portugal began at 18. He made an immediate impact, scoring his first goal at UEFA Euro 2004 and playing a crucial role in helping Portugal reach the final, signaling the rise of a global soccer icon on the international stage.

Cristiano Ronaldo's journey on the international stage blossomed in 2006 when he played in his first World Cup, contributing significantly to Portugal's impressive fourth-place finish. His leadership qualities were further recognized in 2008 when he became the full captain of the Portuguese national team. Under his captaincy, Portugal participated in four European Championships (2008, 2012, 2016, 2020) and three FIFA World Cups (2014, 2018, 2022), showcasing his enduring talent and leadership on the global stage.

Skills & Playing Style

Ronaldo's natural right-footedness and exceptional versatility made him an asset in multiple positions on the field. However, he preferred playing as a forward, where he could best utilize his goal-scoring prowess. This positional preference played a significant role in his development into one of soccer's most prolific scorers.

Furthermore, his physical attributes also set him apart. Celebrated for his lightning speed, he has been recorded reaching speeds of up to 20.9 miles per hour (33.6 kilometers per hour), marking him as one of the fastest players in the sport.

On the pitch, Ronaldo's aerial skills are unparalleled, highlighted by his remarkable record of scoring 145 goals with his head across his tenures at five clubs and the Portugal national team. This ability was vividly showcased in the 2012-13 UEFA Champions League when Ronaldo, playing for Real Madrid, achieved his highest recorded jump of 9 feet 7 inches (2.93m) against Manchester United. Considering his height of 6 feet 2 inches (1.87m), this leap translated to an incredible vertical leap of approximately 41.7 inches (1.06m).

Mastering the art of the 'knuckleball' free kick, Ronaldo has brought an unpredictable element to his game, with 60 free-kick goals. By striking the ball to minimize spin, he created an erratic movement in the air, making it challenging for goalkeepers to predict and defend. His free kicks, often exceeding speeds of 80 miles per hour (130 kilometers per hour), led to some of the most spectacular goals in his career.

Ronaldo has shared the pitch with several notable players on the soccer field. While at Manchester United, he formed formidable partnerships with Wayne Rooney, Ryan Giggs, and Paul Scholes, contributing to the team's Premier League and Champions League successes. At Real Madrid, he played alongside stars like Sergio Ramos, Luka Modrić, and Karim Benzema. Additionally, his international rivalry with Lionel Messi, representing Portugal and Argentina, respectively, has led to iconic clashes in soccer history.

Among his numerous memorable goals, one stands out for his sheer audacity and skill. In a Champions League quarter-final match against Juventus, Ronaldo scored a stunning bicycle kick goal, hailed as one of the most spectacular goals in the tournament's history.

Cristiano Ronaldo's career has been marked by numerous records, but one of the most significant is his achievement of 807 career goals, surpassing Josef Bican's long-standing record. This milestone established Ronaldo as the highest-ever goal scorer in the history of men's soccer, a fitting accolade for one of the greatest players the sport has ever seen.

In addition, his precision isn't limited to open play. He has scored 140 penalty kicks in his career, spanning his time at Sporting CP, Manchester United, Real Madrid, Juventus, and the Portuguese national team. This achievement is a testament to his composure and skill under pressure.

Throughout his career, Ronaldo has continually adapted his playing style. He started as a winger at Manchester United, focusing on delivering crosses. He then transitioned to a more central striker role at Real Madrid, emphasizing goal-scoring. At Juventus, he combined his role as a target man with active dribbling and crossing, showcasing his versatility and commitment to evolving as a player.

Mentorship

Ronaldo's role as a mentor has been instrumental in the development of younger talents. At Manchester United and Real Madrid, he has nurtured players such as Danny Welbeck, Federico Macheda, Lucas Vázquez, and Marco Asensio, boosting their confidence and aiding their growth in top-level soccer.

In turn, Ronaldo acknowledges the mentors who played a crucial role in his own development, including coaches from Sporting CP and Manchester United. Sir Alex Ferguson, in particular, provided invaluable guidance, and assistant manager Carlos Queiroz was instrumental in shaping Ronaldo into a top-level soccerer.

Training, Diet & Mental Fitness

Ronaldo's success is underpinned by a rigorous training regimen. He trains five times a week, with each session lasting 3 to 4 hours and encompassing a mix of cardio exercises, weight training, soccer drills, and high-intensity interval training. This intense routine is supplemented by core strength exercises, swimming, and Pilates, ensuring his body's balance, recovery, and flexibility.

In addition to physical training, Ronaldo places a strong emphasis on maintaining a meticulously planned diet. Consisting of multiple small meals a day, it focuses on proteins, carbohydrates, and healthy fats. He prioritizes lean meats, whole grains, fresh fruits, and vegetables while steering clear of sugary foods and alcohol.

Beyond the physical and dietary aspects, Ronaldo incorporates mental exercises into his regimen. Meditation and visualization techniques are integral to his routine, enhancing his focus, calmness under pressure, and ability to visualize successful outcomes on the field.

While Ronaldo's career has not been without its challenges, marked by significant injuries such as an ankle injury during the 2008 UEFA European Championship and a knee injury at Real Madrid in 2014, his resilience and determination have seen him swiftly recover and maintain a high-performance level. Despite setbacks like a thigh injury in 2019 and a period of COVID-19 isolation in 2020, Ronaldo's ambition to continue playing at the highest level into his late 30s is a testament to his dedication to maintaining peak physical condition and performance, underscoring his relentless pursuit of excellence in soccer.

Personal Life & Interests

Cristiano Ronaldo's life significantly changed in 2016 when he met Georgina Rodriguez in Madrid while she was working as a shop assistant at Gucci. Since then, they have built a life together, expanding their family with the arrival of twins Eva and Mateo in 2017 via surrogacy, followed by their daughter Alana Martina later that year.

Family remains at the heart of Ronaldo's life, emphasizing the importance of family values. As a devoted father, he cares for his children, including his firstborn, Cristiano Jr., born in June 2010, over whom he has full custody. Ronaldo dedicates quality time to his children and partner, engaging in simple yet meaningful activities.

His love for travel has taken him and his family to stunning destinations worldwide, from the vibrant nightlife of Ibiza and Miami to the serene beauty of the Maldives and his hometown, Madeira.

An avid animal lover, Ronaldo is fond of dogs, including breeds like bulldogs and labrador retrievers. He often shares his affection for his canine companions on social media, reflecting his softer side and love for animals.

Cristiano Ronaldo's multifaceted personality and career are further highlighted by his proficiency in several languages. His linguistic abilities in English, Spanish, and Italian, in addition to his native Portuguese, have greatly facilitated his international soccer career. This skill allows him to connect more deeply with fans, teammates, and friends from diverse backgrounds and cultures.

Ronaldo's circle of close friends includes personalities from various fields, reflecting his wide-reaching influence and connections beyond soccer. These friends include former Manchester United teammates Patrice Evra and Rio Ferdinand, UFC fighter Conor McGregor, and actor Dwayne 'The Rock' Johnson.

Cristiano Ronaldo's life off the soccer pitch is as eventful and diverse as his career, encompassing various interests and activities. His involvement in the world of poker extends beyond a mere pastime, as he has participated in professional poker tournaments and promotional events, focusing more on enjoyment and brand promotion than significant monetary gains.

Music also forms an integral part of Ronaldo's life. He is frequently seen at concerts by artists like Rihanna and Jennifer Lopez, sharing his music preferences on social  media. His global prominence has led to collaborations with musicians, including appearances in music videos and promotional campaigns, such as those for Ricky Martin.

Each facet of Ronaldo's life, from his career achievements to his personal interests and family values, paints the picture of a multifaceted individual whose impact and legacy extend far beyond the soccer field.

Fashion & Luxury

Ronaldo's interest in fashion is evident through his active participation in prominent fashion events in cities like Paris and Milan. This involvement showcases not only his prowess on the soccer field but also his sense of style and engagement with the fashion world.

His hairstyle, a frequent topic of discussion, has become almost as iconic as his soccer skills. From sleek combed-back looks to edgy spiked designs, Ronaldo's hair has set trends, with the zigzag pattern during the 2014 World Cup standing out. Beyond being a mere fashion statement, his hairstyles are a form of personal expression, widely imitated and extending his influence beyond sports.

In addition to his fashion-forward image, Ronaldo's passion for luxury vehicles is reflected in his impressive collection. This includes exclusive sports cars such as the Bugatti Veyron, Lamborghini Aventador, Ferrari F12, and the standout $3 million Bugatti Chiron. The collection not only showcases his love for high-performance automobiles but also exemplifies his taste for style and the finer things in life.

Complementing his extravagant lifestyle, Ronaldo's ownership of a private jet adds to his ability to manage a hectic schedule. This enables him to balance professional commitments and personal life efficiently, emphasizing his commitment to maintaining a seamless and luxurious lifestyle.

Off the Field Ventures

Cristiano Ronaldo's journey into the world of fragrances marked a unique extension of his brand. In 2017, he introduced 'CR7 Fragrances,' unveiling the 'CR7 Eau de Toilette'—a contemporary, sporty scent mirroring his distinctive style and charisma.

Even before attaining global fame, Ronaldo made an early foray into marketing. In a 2003 television commercial for 'Super Bock,' a Portuguese clothing brand, he showcased one of his initial brand endorsements, providing a glimpse into his early steps in the realm of endorsements.

Ronaldo's worldwide allure is evident in a multitude of brand endorsements. As an ambassador for Clear Shampoo and Herbalife, he champions hair care and health and wellness products. Simultaneously, he represents TAG Heuer, a prestigious Swiss watch brand, and collaborates with DAZN, a sports streaming service, to boost their sports coverage.

Venturing further into entrepreneurship, Ronaldo has left his mark on the travel industry, associating with American Tourister and co-owning CR7 Hotels in partnership with the Pestana Hotel Group. Additionally, he endorses MTG's healthcare and fitness products, exemplifying his dedication to a lifestyle encompassing health, luxury, and business.

Cristiano Ronaldo's life and career, punctuated by milestones and personal interests, narrate the tale of a man who surpasses the confines of soccer.

In a monumental move, Ronaldo secured a lifetime endorsement deal with Nike in 2016, valued at a staggering $1 billion. This historic agreement, following in the footsteps of athletes like LeBron James and Michael Jordan, underscores his unparalleled marketing influence.

Ronaldo's social media presence alone contributed a remarkable $474 million in value for Nike in 2016, a testament to his immense commercial prowess.

Philanthropy

Cristiano Ronaldo's impact extends beyond the soccer field through his philanthropic efforts. In 2017, he donated €1.5 million to fund a pediatric hospital in Madeira, his hometown. Recognized as the world's most charitable sportsperson in 2015, he donated €5 million to the earthquake relief efforts in Nepal. His generosity also includes significant contributions to children's charities, funding schools in war zones, and supporting organizations like Save the Children.

In response to the global challenge posed by the COVID-19 pandemic, Ronaldo, alongside his agent Jorge Mendes, stepped up to support hospitals in Portugal. They donated significant funds for critical care beds and medical equipment, playing a crucial role in the fight against the pandemic.

Ronaldo's contributions have also had a significant impact on his hometown of Madeira. His donations to local hospitals, the establishment of the CR7 Museum, involvement in youth development programs, and charitable activities through the Cristiano Ronaldo Foundation have positively influenced healthcare, tourism, education, and youth empowerment in the region.

In addition, his commitment to making a difference has seen him involved in campaigns for blood and bone marrow donation. Using his global influence, he raises awareness about these crucial health issues. His personal choice to remain tattoo-free is influenced by his dedication to regularly donating blood, enabling him to avoid the waiting periods often required following tattooing.

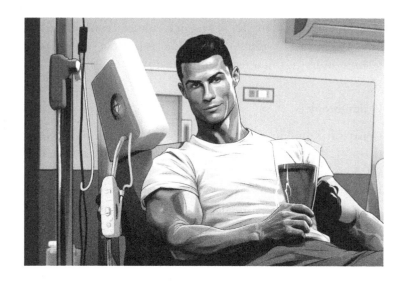

Through his dedication to soccer, rigorous training, and generous philanthropy, Cristiano Ronaldo has not only etched his name in the annals of sporting history but has also emerged as a role model, demonstrating the impact a global sports icon can have both on and off the field.

Online Presence

Cristiano Ronaldo's dominance in the digital realm is unparalleled. With over 612 million followers, he reigns supreme as the most-followed individual, male figure, sports personality, and European personality on Instagram. His online presence extends beyond Instagram, with a highly-viewed Wikipedia page for a male athlete and a prominent position among the most-followed personalities on Twitter.

What sets Ronaldo apart is not just the numbers but his genuine connection with fans. Known for his accessibility, he readily fulfills requests for selfies and autographs, fostering a personal bond with supporters. His active engagement on social media goes beyond mere postings;

he personally responds to comments and messages. This approachable demeanor underscores his deep appreciation for the global fan base that supports him, emphasizing a commitment to reciprocating the admiration he receives.

In the digital landscape, Ronaldo's popularity is not just about statistics; it's a testament to his global influence and the widespread interest he commands. Whether interacting with fans or making waves on various online platforms, Ronaldo's digital footprint showcases a level of engagement and connection that goes beyond traditional notions of sports stardom.

Fun & Random Ronaldo Tidbits

• From a young age, Ronaldo looked up to the Brazilian soccer legends Ronaldinho and Ronaldo Nazário. He admired their extraordinary skills and the legacy they left in soccer, often citing them as his idols who inspired him to carve his path in the soccer world.

• Raised in a devout Catholic family, Ronaldo's faith has been an integral part of his life. While he maintains a private stance on his religious beliefs, his actions, such as making the sign of the cross before games, indicate a deep personal faith.

• Known for his meticulous nature, Ronaldo follows a set of superstitious habits, including stepping onto the pitch with his right foot first and styling his hair before each match. These rituals have become integral to his pre-game routine.

• Upon joining Manchester United in 2003, Ronaldo's limited English necessitated a translator for communication, particularly with Sir Alex Ferguson. Over time, he overcame the language barrier, although he humorously admits to still finding Ferguson's Scottish accent challenging to understand.

• Ronaldo's association with the iconic number 7 jersey at Manchester United has become a significant part of his identity. He inherited this number, which club legends like George Best, Eric Cantona, and David Beckham had worn. He made it synonymous with his legacy.

• In 2009, Real Madrid, recognizing Ronaldo's value, took extraordinary measures to protect their investment; the club insured his legs for a reported sum of around €100 million, underscoring the high esteem in which he was held.

• One of the most iconic elements of Ronaldo's persona is his signature "Siu" celebration, which he debuted in 2013 during a match with Real Madrid against Chelsea. This dynamic jump, accompanied by a confident shout of "Siu" – meaning "Yes" in Spanish – became synonymous with his moments of triumph and joy upon scoring.

• On the field, Ronaldo's competitive nature has occasionally led to controversy. His intensity and passion have resulted in several red cards and debates over his sportsmanship, particularly his reactions to referee decisions and confrontations with opponents.

• In 2017, Ronaldo faced accusations of tax evasion in Spain, involving €14.7 million related to image rights income. He settled the case in 2019, accepting a suspended jail sentence and agreeing to pay €18.8 million in fines, avoiding jail time.

• In the virtual world of FIFA 18, Ronaldo was recognized as the highest-rated player, with an overall rating of 99%, showcasing his prominence in the sport.

• In 2020, as reported by Forbes, Ronaldo made history as the first active team sport athlete to surpass $1 billion in career earnings.

• The CR7 Museum in Funchal, Madeira, inaugurated in 2013, pays homage to Ronaldo's illustrious career. It houses a collection of his trophies, medals, photographs  from his childhood, and memorabilia from significant matches, offering fans a comprehensive look at his journey.

• Ronaldo's fame is reflected in his representation as a waxwork at Madame Tussauds in London, joining soccer legends like Steven Gerrard, Pelé, and David Beckham. This honor celebrates his achievements and popularity in the realm of sports.

3

TRIVIA QUESTIONS

Dive into the intriguing world of Cristiano Ronaldo with this trivia, where each question unveils a captivating facet of the soccer legend's journey. Test your knowledge and discover the untold stories behind the records and achievements that define Ronaldo's remarkable life on and off the pitch.

1. What is Cristiano Ronaldo's full name and where was he born?

a) Cristiano Ronaldo de Silva, Lisbon, Portugal

b) Cristiano Ronaldo dos Santos Aveiro, Madeira, Portugal

c) Cristiano Ronaldo Fernandes, Porto, Portugal

d) Cristiano Ronaldo Soares, Faro, Portugal

2. Cristiano Ronaldo is the youngest child of how many siblings?

a) Two

b) Three

c) Four

d) Five

3. What was Cristiano Ronaldo's father's profession?

a) Teacher

b) Soccer coach

c) Municipal gardener and part-time kit man

d) Mechanic

4. What role did Ronaldo's mother play in his early soccer career?

a) She was his first coach

b) She managed his early contracts

c) She encouraged his talent and took him to training sessions

d) She funded his soccer academy fees

5. What is Ronaldo's older brother, Hugo, known for?

a) Being a professional soccerer

b) Working on Ronaldo's CR7 brand and museum

c) Managing Ronaldo's finances

d) Coaching in the youth academy

6. What are Cristiano Ronaldo's sisters' names and professions?

a) Elma (fashion designer) and Liliana Cátia (lawyer)

b) Elma (manages CR7 fashion brand) and Liliana Cátia (singer)

c) Elma (teacher) and Liliana Cátia (architect)

d) Elma (businesswoman) and Liliana Cátia (chef)

7. After whom was Cristiano Ronaldo named?

a) Ronaldinho, a soccerer

b) Ronald Reagan, an actor

c) Ronaldo Nazário, a soccerer

d) Ronald McDonald, a fictional character

8. What were Ronaldo's childhood nicknames?

a) 'Speedy' and 'Goal Machine'

b) 'Cristy' and 'Rocket'

c) 'Cry Baby' and 'Little Bee'

d) 'Junior' and 'Flash'

9. At what age did Cristiano Ronaldo start playing soccer and for which team?

a) 6, Porto

b) 8, Andorinha

c) 10, Sporting CP

d) 12, Benfica

10. Why was Cristiano Ronaldo expelled from school at age 14?

a) Poor grades

b) Fighting with classmates

c) Throwing a chair at his teacher

d) Skipping classes to play soccer

11. What medical condition did Cristiano Ronaldo have at the age of 15, requiring heart surgery?

a) Arrhythmia

b) Tachycardia

c) Hypertension

d) Cardiomyopathy

12. When did Cristiano Ronaldo begin his professional soccer career?

a) 2000

b) 2001

c) 2002

d) 2003

13. Which club signed Cristiano Ronaldo in 2003, for a then-record fee for a teenager?

a) Barcelona

b) Manchester United

c) Real Madrid

d) AC Milan

14. What signature move is Cristiano Ronaldo known for during his time at Manchester United?

a) The Ronaldo Turn

b) The Ronaldo Chop

c) The Ronaldo Spin

d) The Ronaldo Dash

15. How many consecutive Premier League titles did Ronaldo win with Manchester United?

a) One

b) Two

c) Three

d) Four

16. In which season did Ronaldo help Manchester United win the UEFA Champions League?

a) 2005-06

b) 2006-07

c) 2007-08

d) 2008-09

17. When did Ronaldo win his first FIFA Club World Cup with Manchester United?

a) 2006

b) 2007

c) 2008

d) 2009

18. In which year did Cristiano Ronaldo win his first Ballon d'Or?

a) 2006

b) 2007

c) 2008

d) 2009

19. For how much was Cristiano Ronaldo transferred to Real Madrid in 2009, setting a world record at the time?

a) £60 million

b) £70 million

c) £80 million

d) £90 million

20. How many seasons did Ronaldo spend at Real Madrid, becoming the club's all-time leading scorer?

a) Seven

b) Eight

c) Nine

d) Ten

21. How many Champions League titles did Cristiano Ronaldo win during his time at Real Madrid?

a) Two

b) Three

c) Four

d) Five

22. Where was Ronaldo ranked in the 'World Player of the Decade 2000s'?

a) First

b) Second

c) Third

d) Fourth

23. In which season did Ronaldo win his first trophy with Real Madrid?

a) 2009-10

b) 2010-11

c) 2011-12

d) 2012-13

24. Which title did Ronaldo secure with Real Madrid in the 2011-12 season?

a) Champions League

b) La Liga

c) Copa del Rey

d) Supercopa de España

25. What did Ronaldo win with Real Madrid in the 2012-13 season?

a) Champions League

b) La Liga

c) Copa del Rey

d) Supercopa de España

26. In which season did Ronaldo win his second Ballon d'Or?

a) 2011-12

b) 2012-13

c) 2013-14

d) 2014-15

27. How many goals did Ronaldo score in the Champions League in the 2013-14 season, setting a record?

a) 15

b) 16

c) 17

d) 18

28. What did Ronaldo win in 2014, along with his third Ballon d'Or?

a) La Liga

b) Copa del Rey

c) Champions League

d) FIFA Club World Cup

29. In which year did Ronaldo win his third Champions League with Real Madrid, scoring the winning penalty in the final?

a) 2014

b) 2015

c) 2016

d) 2017

30. What achievements did Ronaldo earn in the season following his third Champions League win with Real Madrid?

a) Fourth Ballon d'Or, La Liga title, Champions League, Club World Cup

b) Third Ballon d'Or, Copa del Rey, Supercopa de España

c) Fifth Ballon d'Or, La Liga title, Europa League

d) Fourth Ballon d'Or, Copa del Rey, Champions League

31. What were the major achievements of Ronaldo's last season with Real Madrid in 2017-18?

a) Fifth Ballon d'Or and fourth Champions League title

b) Fourth Ballon d'Or and fifth Champions League title

c) Fifth Ballon d'Or and fifth Champions League title

d) Sixth Ballon d'Or and fifth Champions League title

32. Ronaldo set a record as the first player to win how many UEFA Champions League titles?

a) Three

b) Four

c) Five

d) Six

33. When Ronaldo transferred to Juventus in 2018, what record did he leave behind at Real Madrid?

a) All-time top goal scorer with 30 or more goals in five consecutive seasons

b) All-time top goal scorer with 40 or more goals in six consecutive seasons

c) All-time top goal scorer with 30 or more goals in six consecutive seasons

d) All-time top goal scorer with 50 or more goals in four consecutive seasons

34. At what age did Ronaldo begin his international career with Portugal, and when did he score his first goal?

a) 16 years old, UEFA Euro 2004

b) 18 years old, UEFA Euro 2004

c) 20 years old, FIFA World Cup 2006

d) 18 years old, FIFA World Cup 2006

35. In which year did Ronaldo play in his first World Cup, and what was Portugal's finish?

a) 2004, semi-finals

b) 2006, fourth place

c) 2008, quarter-finals

d) 2010, round of 16

36. Since what year has Ronaldo been the full captain of Portugal, and in how many European Championships and FIFA World Cups has he participated since then?

a) 2008, four European Championships and three FIFA World Cups

b) 2006, three European Championships and four FIFA World Cups

c) 2010, four European Championships and four FIFA World Cups

d) 2004, five European Championships and three FIFA World Cups

37. Which Brazilian soccer legends did Ronaldo admire during his youth?

a) Pele and Zico

b) Ronaldinho and Ronaldo Nazário

c) Rivaldo and Romário

d) Cafu and Roberto Carlos

38. What is Ronaldo's preferred position on the field?

a) Winger

b) Forward

c) Midfielder

d) Defender

39. What is Ronaldo's recorded top speed on the pitch?

a) 17.9 miles per hour

b) 19.2 miles per hour

c) 20.9 miles per hour

d) 22.4 miles per hour

40. How tall is Cristiano Ronaldo and what is his vertical leap?

a) 6 feet, 28.7 inches

b) 6 feet 1 inch, 30.7 inches

c) 6 feet 2 inches, 32.7 inches

d) 6 feet 2 inches, 41.7 inches

41. What is the name of the free kick technique mastered by Ronaldo, which involves minimizing spin on the ball?

a) The Rocket Kick

b) The Curveball Kick

c) The Knuckleball Free Kick

d) The Spinball Kick

42. How many penalty kicks has Ronaldo scored in his professional club and international career?

a) 100

b) 120

c) 140

d) 160

43. How many hat-tricks has Ronaldo scored in his professional career for club and country?

a) 40

b) 50

c) 60

d) 70

44. What does Cristiano Ronaldo's signature "Siu" celebration mean in Spanish?

a) Jump

b) Victory

c) Yes

d) Amazing

45. As of the given facts, how many career goals has Cristiano Ronaldo achieved, surpassing Josef Bican's record?

a) 785

b) 795

c) 807

d) 815

46. How many goals has Ronaldo scored with his head across his tenures at five clubs and the Portugal national team?

a) 125

b) 135

c) 145

d) 155

47. What is Ronaldo's highest recorded jump height, achieved in the UEFA Champions League against Manchester United?

a) 8 feet 9 inches

b) 9 feet 7 inches

c) 10 feet 2 inches

d) 10 feet 6 inches

48. Against which team did Ronaldo score a celebrated bicycle kick goal in a Champions League quarter-final match?

a) Barcelona

b) Juventus

c) Bayern Munich

d) Paris Saint-Germain

49. What was the reported sum for which Real Madrid insured Ronaldo's legs in 2009?

a) Around €50 million

b) Around €75 million

c) Around €100 million

d) Around €125 million

50. How long does each of Ronaldo's training sessions typically last?

a) 1 to 2 hours

b) 2 to 3 hours

c) 3 to 4 hours

d) 4 to 5 hours

51. What additional exercises does Ronaldo incorporate into his training regimen for balance, recovery, and flexibility?

a) Yoga, Running, and Weightlifting

b) Core Strength Exercises, Swimming, and Pilates

c) Boxing, Cycling, and Aerobics

d) Martial Arts, Dance, and Sprinting

52. How is Cristiano Ronaldo's diet planned?

a) High in protein, low in carbs, no fruits or vegetables

b) Multiple small meals a day, rich in protein, carbohydrates, and healthy fats

c) One large meal a day, low in fats, high in protein

d) Vegetarian diet, excluding all forms of meat

53. What mental exercises does Ronaldo include in his training regimen?

a) Hypnosis and Deep Breathing

b) Meditation and Visualization Techniques

c) Cognitive Behavioral Therapy and Positive Affirmations

d) Neuro-Linguistic Programming and Mindfulness

54. How much did Ronaldo donate to fund a pediatric hospital in Madeira in 2017?

a) €500,000

b) €1 million

c) €1.5 million

d) €2 million

55. In which year was Ronaldo named the world's most charitable sportsperson?

a) 2012

b) 2015

c) 2018

d) 2020

56. Which children's charity does Ronaldo frequently contribute to?

a) UNICEF

b) Save the Children

c) World Vision

d) Plan International

57. What campaigns has Ronaldo been involved in to raise awareness?

a) Cancer research and mental health

b) Blood donation and bone marrow donation

c) Climate change and environmental protection

d) Animal rights and veganism

58. Why has Cristiano Ronaldo chosen not to have any tattoos?

a) Personal preference

b) Religious beliefs

c) Commitment to regularly donating blood

d) Allergic to tattoo ink

59. What did Ronaldo and his agent Jorge Mendes donate during the COVID-19 pandemic?

a) Funds for vaccines and research

b) Funds for critical care beds and medical equipment

c) Food and supplies for those affected

d) Personal protective equipment for healthcare workers

60. What religious gesture does Ronaldo often make before games?

a) Making the cross sign

b) Kneeling and praying

c) Bowing towards Mecca

d) Meditating silently

61. What is the name of Cristiano Ronaldo's signature fragrance line, launched in 2017?

a) CR7 Elegance

b) CR7 Fragrances

c) Ronaldo Essence

d) Cristiano Scents

62. In which year did Ronaldo appear in a television commercial for 'Super Bock,' marking one of his earliest brand endorsements?

a) 2001

b) 2003

c) 2005

d) 2007

63. How much in image rights income was Ronaldo accused of evading in taxes by Spanish authorities in 2017?

a) €10.7 million

b) €12.7 million

c) €14.7 million

d) €16.7 million

64. Ronaldo's competitive nature on the field has led to several red cards and criticism. What aspects of his behavior have been debated?

a) Goal celebrations and interviews

b) Reactions to referee decisions and confrontations with opponents

c) Team selection and coaching criticism

d) Media interactions and sponsorship deals

65. Which brands does Ronaldo represent as a global ambassador?

a) Adidas and Gatorade

b) Clear Shampoo and Herbalife

c) Puma and Red Bull

d) Under Armour and Monster Energy

66. Which high-end Swiss watch brand and sports streaming service does Ronaldo represent?

a) Rolex and ESPN

b) TAG Heuer and DAZN

c) Omega and Sky Sports

d) Breitling and Hulu Sports

67. In addition to his soccer career, Ronaldo has business ventures in various industries. Which of these does he not have a collaboration with?

a) American Tourister

b) CR7 Hotels with the Pestana Hotel Group

c) MTG's healthcare and fitness products

d) A personal airline company

68. Which World Cup saw Ronaldo sporting a zigzag hairstyle, becoming a trend among fans?

a) 2010 World Cup

b) 2014 World Cup

c) 2018 World Cup

d) 2022 World Cup

69. Which of these luxury cars is not in Cristiano Ronaldo's collection?

a) Bugatti Veyron

b) Lamborghini Aventador

c) Ferrari F12

d) McLaren P1

70. Since when has Cristiano Ronaldo been under a lifetime endorsement deal with Nike, and how much is it valued at?

a) Since 2014, valued at $500 million

b) Since 2016, valued at $1 billion

c) Since 2018, valued at $750 million

d) Since 2020, valued at $1.5 billion

71. What is the purpose of Ronaldo's private jet?

a) To attend charity events only

b) To travel for professional soccer matches and personal commitments

c) To participate in air races

d) For luxury tourism business

72. When was the CR7 Museum in Funchal, Madeira, inaugurated, and what does it showcase?

a) 2010, showcasing his luxury car collection

b) 2013, showcasing his career achievements and personal life

c) 2015, showcasing his fashion and fragrance lines

d) 2018, showcasing his real estate investments

73. How many free-kick goals has Ronaldo scored in his professional career?

a) 40

b) 50

c) 60

d) 70

74. When did Cristiano Ronaldo's relationship with Georgina Rodriguez begin?

a) 2014

b) 2015

c) 2016

d) 2017

75. How many children does Cristiano Ronaldo have, and how was his second set of children born?

a) Three, via surrogacy

b) Four, with two born via surrogacy

c) Five, with one adopted

d) Four, all naturally born

76. What does Cristiano Ronaldo emphasize as an important aspect of his life?

a) His car collection

b) Fashion and style

c) Family values

d) His soccer legacy

77. What milestone did Ronaldo achieve in 2020 in terms of career earnings?

a) $500 million

b) $750 million

c) $1 billion

d) $1.5 billion

78. Which of the following is not listed as one of Ronaldo's favorite vacation spots?

a) Ibiza

b) Miami

c) Tokyo

d) Maldives

79. Which fashion events does Ronaldo actively participate in?

a) New York and London Fashion Weeks

b) Paris and Milan Fashion Weeks

c) Berlin and Sydney Fashion Weeks

d) Toronto and São Paulo Fashion Weeks

80. When did Cristiano Ronaldo make his debut for Al Nassr?

a) December 2022

b) January 2023

c) February 2023

d) March 2023

81. What is Ronaldo's involvement in professional poker tournaments?

a) Primarily for significant monetary gains

b) Mainly for enjoyment and brand promotion

c) As a professional poker player

d) For charity fundraising events

82. Which musicians have Ronaldo collaborated with, as reflected in his appearances in music videos and promotional campaigns?

a) Beyoncé and Jay-Z

b) Ricky Martin and Shakira

c) Ricky Martin and Jennifer Lopez

d) Ed Sheeran and Taylor Swift

83. Which notable players did Ronaldo share the pitch with during his time at Manchester United?

a) David Beckham, Ryan Giggs, and Paul Scholes

b) Wayne Rooney, Ryan Giggs, and Paul Scholes

c) Nemanja Vidić, Rio Ferdinand, and Wayne Rooney

d) Gary Neville, David Beckham, and Roy Keane

84. Who were Ronaldo's teammates at Real Madrid, contributing to the team's success?

a) Gareth Bale, Karim Benzema, and James Rodríguez

b) Sergio Ramos, Luka Modrić, and Karim Benzema

c) Iker Casillas, Marcelo, and Toni Kroos

d) Isco, Raphael Varane, and Keylor Navas

85. What is the estimated value of Ronaldo's contract with Al Nassr, signed in 2023?

a) More than 150 million euros

b) More than 200 million euros

c) More than 250 million euros

d) More than 300 million euros

86. Which significant injuries has Ronaldo faced throughout his career?

a) Ankle, knee, thigh injuries, and COVID-19 isolation

b) Shoulder, back, hamstring injuries, and flu

c) Concussion, wrist, hip injuries, and malaria

d) Elbow, shin, calf injuries, and chickenpox

87. In the digital realm, what distinguishes Cristiano Ronaldo's Wikipedia page?

a) Most-edited page

b) Most-viewed page for a male athlete

c) Longest page in terms of content

d) Highest-rated page by users

88. Who are some of the young talents Ronaldo has mentored at Manchester United and Real Madrid?

a) Danny Welbeck, Federico Macheda, Lucas Vázquez, Marco Asensio

b) Jesse Lingard, Marcus Rashford, Álvaro Morata, Isco

c) Adnan Januzaj, Ángel Di María, Casemiro, Nacho

d) Javier Hernández, Mateo Kovačić, Dani Carvajal, Jesé

89. Which famous personalities are among Cristiano Ronaldo's close friends?

a) Lionel Messi, Neymar Jr., and LeBron James

b) Patrice Evra, Rio Ferdinand, Conor McGregor, Dwayne 'The Rock' Johnson

c) David Beckham, Cristiano Jr., and Khabib Nurmagomedov

d) Paul Pogba, Marcelo, and Kevin Hart

90. How is Ronaldo known to interact with fans?

a) Rarely interacts or grants requests for selfies and autographs

b) Often grants requests for selfies and autographs

c) Only interacts with fans at official events

d) Primarily interacts through his management team

91. In addition to Portuguese, what other languages is Cristiano Ronaldo proficient in?

a) German, French, and Russian

b) English, Spanish, and Italian

c) Dutch, Japanese, and Arabic

d) Swedish, Chinese, and Greek

92. How has Ronaldo impacted his hometown of Madeira, Portugal?

a) By building a sports complex and a university

b) Through donations, the CR7 Museum, and youth programs

c) By establishing a soccer academy and a theme park

d) Through real estate development and creating job opportunities

93. What type of animals is Ronaldo known to be an avid lover of?

a) Cats

b) Horses

c) Dogs

d) Birds

94. Who were Ronaldo's early mentors?

a) Pep Guardiola and Zinedine Zidane

b) José Mourinho and Carlo Ancelotti

c) Sir Alex Ferguson and Carlos Queiroz

d) Arsène Wenger and Frank Rijkaard

95. What was Ronaldo's overall rating in FIFA 18, making him the highest-rated player?

a) 97%

b) 98%

c) 99%

d) 100%

96. Which iconic jersey number is associated with Cristiano Ronaldo at Manchester United?

a) Number 7

b) Number 10

c) Number 11

d) Number 9

97. What type of superstitious habits is Ronaldo known for?

a) Wearing the same socks for every match

b) Stepping onto the pitch with his right foot first

c) Always playing with a wristband

d) Listening to the same song before every match

98. Upon joining Manchester United, what language barrier did Ronaldo face?

a) Difficulty in understanding Spanish

b) Limited grasp of English

c) Inability to speak French

d) Challenges with Italian

99. Cristiano Ronaldo became the fourth soccerer to have what honor at Madame Tussauds in London?

a) A documentary film

b) A waxwork

c) A bronze statue

d) An exclusive gallery

100. What record does Ronaldo hold on Instagram?

a) Most-followed athlete

b) Most-followed European personality

c) Both of the above

d) Most likes on a single post

101. How has Ronaldo's playing style evolved throughout his career?

a) From a striker to a winger

b) From a midfielder to a forward

c) From a winger to a central striker

d) From a defender to a midfielder

4

TRIVIA ANSWERS

Now, let's reveal the correct answers to the trivia questions, shedding light on the key moments and milestones that have shaped the soccer icon's extraordinary journey.

1. b) Cristiano Ronaldo dos Santos Aveiro, Madeira, Portugal

2. c) Four

3. c) Municipal gardener and part-time kit man

4. c) She encouraged his talent and took him to training sessions

5. b) Working on Ronaldo's CR7 brand and museum

6. b) Elma (manages CR7 fashion brand) and Liliana Cátia (singer)

7. b) Ronald Reagan, an actor

8. c) 'Cry Baby' and 'Little Bee'

9. b) 8, Andorinha

10. c) Throwing a chair at his teacher

11. b) Tachycardia

12. c) 2002

13. b) Manchester United

14. b) The Ronaldo Chop

15. c) Three

16. c) 2007-08

17. c) 2008

18. c) 2008

19. c) £80 million

20. c) Nine

21. c) Four

22. c) Third

23. b) 2010-11

24. b) La Liga

25. d) Supercopa de España

26. c) 2013-14

27. c) 17

28. d) FIFA Club World Cup

29. c) 2016

30. a) Fourth Ballon d'Or, La Liga title, Champions League, Club World Cup

31. c) Fifth Ballon d'Or and fifth Champions League title

32. c) Five

33. c) All-time top goal scorer with 30 or more goals in six consecutive seasons

34. b) 18 years old, UEFA Euro 2004

35. b) 2006, fourth place

36. a) 2008, four European Championships and three FIFA World Cups

37. b) Ronaldinho and Ronaldo Nazário

38. b) Forward

39. c) 20.9 miles per hour

40. d) 6 feet 2 inches, 41.7 inches

41. c) The Knuckleball Free Kick

42. c) 140

43. c) 60

44. c) Yes

45. c) 807

46. c) 145

47. b) 9 feet 7 inches

48. b) Juventus

49. c) Around €100 million

50. c) 3 to 4 hours

51. b) Core Strength Exercises, Swimming, and Pilates

52. b) Multiple small meals a day, rich in protein, carbohydrates, and healthy fats

53. b) Meditation and Visualization Techniques

54. c) €1.5 million

55. b) 2015

56. b) Save the Children

57. b) Blood donation and bone marrow donation

58. c) Commitment to regularly donating blood

59. b) Funds for critical care beds and medical equipment

60. a) Making the cross sign

61. b) CR7 Fragrances

62. b) 2003

63. c) €14.7 million

64. b) Reactions to referee decisions and confrontations with opponents

65. b) Clear Shampoo and Herbalife

66. b) TAG Heuer and DAZN

67. d) A personal airline company

68. b) 2014 World Cup

69. d) McLaren P1

70. b) Since 2016, valued at $1 billion

71. b) To travel for professional soccer matches and personal commitments

72. b) 2013, showcasing his career achievements and personal life

73. c) 60

74. c) 2016

75. b) Four, with two born via surrogacy

76. c) Family values

77. c) $1 billion

78. c) Tokyo

79. b) Paris and Milan Fashion Weeks

80. b) January 2023

81. b) Mainly for enjoyment and brand promotion

82. c) Ricky Martin and Jennifer Lopez

83. b) Wayne Rooney, Ryan Giggs, and Paul Scholes

84. b) Sergio Ramos, Luka Modrić, and Karim Benzema

85. b) More than 200 million euros

86. a) Ankle, knee, thigh injuries, and COVID-19 isolation

87. b) Most-viewed page for a male athlete

88. a) Danny Welbeck, Federico Macheda, Lucas Vázquez, Marco Asensio

89. b) Patrice Evra, Rio Ferdinand, Conor McGregor, Dwayne 'The Rock' Johnson

90. b) Often grants requests for selfies and autographs

91. b) English, Spanish, and Italian

92. b) Through donations, the CR7 Museum, and youth programs

93. c) Dogs

94. c) Sir Alex Ferguson and Carlos Queiroz

95. c) 99%

96. a) Number 7

97. b) Stepping onto the pitch with his right foot first

98. b) Limited grasp of English

99. b) A waxwork

100. c) Both of the above

101. c) From a winger to a central striker

5

RONALDO QUIZ SCORECARD

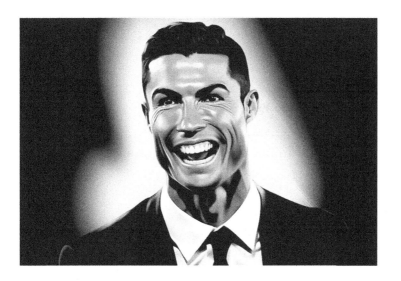

Score ___/101

1-20: Beginner Fan

You're just starting to learn about Ronaldo. Keep exploring his story, and your knowledge will surely grow!

71

21-40: Rising Star

You have a budding understanding of Cristiano Ronaldo. Continue your journey, and you'll uncover even more about this soccer legend!

41-60: In the Game

You're getting to know Ronaldo quite well. Stay curious, and you'll soon be a Ronaldo aficionado!

61-80: Ronaldo Enthusiast

Impressive! You have a solid grasp of Cristiano Ronaldo's career and life. Keep up the good work, and you'll soon be a top expert!

81-100: Ronaldo Expert

Fantastic! Your knowledge about Cristiano Ronaldo is remarkable. You're nearly at the pinnacle of Ronaldo expertise!

101: Ultimate Ronaldo Fan

Incredible! You've achieved the highest score, proving your status as the ultimate Cristiano Ronaldo fan. You truly know CR7 inside and out!

BONUS: FREE MESSI BOOK

Are you ready to delve into the next thrilling book in the series, absolutely free? Get ready to explore the captivating world of yet another soccer legend! Just use your smartphone or tablet to scan the QR code below, then follow the simple prompts to receive the PDF.

Made in the USA
Las Vegas, NV
16 December 2024

14447128R00046